The King
Who Was Late

A Division of The McGraw·Hill Companies

Columbus, Ohio

www.sra4kids.com

SRA/McGraw-Hill

A Division of The **McGraw·Hill** *Companies*

Printed in the United States of America.

Send all inquiries to:
SRA/McGraw-Hill
8787 Orion Place
Columbus, OH 43240-4027

ISBN 0-07-569760-2
4 5 6 7 8 9 DBH 05

The Message

King Ray was late.
"My dear wife might be angry
if I make her wait," he said.
"I must tell her that I will be late."

3

So King Ray told his page:
"Please tell dear Queen Fay that
I may be late
for dinner tonight."

4

His page told Sir Dwight:
"Please tell dear Queen Fay that
King Ray may put on a bright leaf
for dinner tonight."

Sir Dwight told Lord Jay:
"Please tell dear Queen Fay that
King Ray may sail a fancy kite
before dinner tonight."

Lord Jay told the mayor:
"Please tell dear Queen Fay that
King Ray may eat berries on ice
for dinner tonight."

7

The mayor told Lady Grieves:
"Please tell dear Queen Fay that
King Ray may heat some really nice rice
for dinner tonight."

The Answer

Lady Grieves told the maid:
"Please tell dear Queen Fay that
King Ray may invite five greedy mice
to dinner tonight."

The maid told Prince Henry:
"Please tell dear Queen Fay that
King Ray might fight thieves in the field
before dinner tonight."

Prince Henry told Princess Paige:
"Please tell dear Queen Fay that
King Ray may add the right spice
and make a fine dinner tonight."

Princess Paige told dear Queen Fay:
"Dear Queen Fay, King Ray may be late
to dinner tonight.
He does not want you to wait."

Queen Fay answered: "Dear King Ray is always late. I will save him a piece of dinner."